JUST LIKE ME

by Amy G. Koss

The rain was coming down in buckets, and this Saturday promised to be a long, dull day. I wanted to do something fun, so I finally decided to build a robot. Does it sound weird that I wanted to build a robot? That's what both my parents do, and they leave all kinds of robot parts lying around the house!

All through breakfast, I imagined robots in countless sizes, from tiny bugs to gigantic soldiers. Some were round like grapefruits, while others were straight and stiff, like skyscrapers.

A spoon-sized robot would fit snugly on my shoulder, but it would be easy to lose. A huge robot could give me a ride to school in three giant steps, but where would I keep it at night?

Then I had a brilliant idea! I would make the robot my size, and it would talk, think, and act like me as well. It would be another me!

I gathered a bunch of robot parts and some magazines for robot builders, and I started building. When I was finished, I named my robot Jason Too.

All morning, Jason Too and I played games and read stories that we both enjoyed. We both laughed at the same things at the same time. Later, we ate the same kind of sandwich, without tomatoes!

In the afternoon, we decided to watch television. Jason Too stretched out on the couch like I do, with his arms over his head and his feet hanging over one end. There wasn't enough room for both of us, so we agreed to sit upright.

Later, when I went to the kitchen to make popcorn, I tripped over Jason Too's shoes. He had kicked them off in the middle of the hall, just as I had.

"Okay, Jason," I said. "I think we both need to be reprogrammed! I'll stop hogging the couch and leaving my shoes in the middle of the floor, but you have to stop, too. Agreed?" He nodded.

Our favorite show was starting, so Jason Too saved room for me on the couch, while I raced to the kitchen. I made two bowls of popcorn, one for each of us, because I knew he might still hog the popcorn, just like me.